Intermediate 2
English

"1999" Specimen Question Paper
Paper I: Interpretation
Paper II

2000 Exam
Interpretation
Analysis & Appreciation

2001 Exam
Close Reading
Analysis & Appreciation

2002 Exam
Close Reading
Analysis & Appreciation

Specimen Question Paper for Exams in and after 2003
Close Reading
Critical Essay

2003 Exam
Close Reading
Critical Essay

© Scottish Qualifications Authority

All rights reserved. Copying prohibited. No part of this publication may be reproduced, stored in a retrieval system, or transmitted in any form or by any means, electronic, mechanical, photocopying, recording or otherwise.

First exam published in 1999.
Published by
Leckie & Leckie, 8 Whitehill Terrace, St. Andrews, Scotland KY16 8RN
tel: 01334 475656 fax: 01334 477392
enquiries@leckieandleckie.co.uk www.leckieandleckie.co.uk

Leckie & Leckie Project Team: Peter Dennis; John MacPherson; Bruce Ryan; Andrea Smith

ISBN 1-84372-112-0

A CIP Catalogue record for this book is available from the British Library.

Printed in Scotland by Scotprint.

Leckie & Leckie is a division of Granada Learning Limited, part of Granada plc.

Introduction

Dear Student,

This past paper book provides you with the perfect opportunity to put into practice everything you need to know in order to excel in your exams. The range of past papers offers you an invaluable insight into what to expect on the day and will help you to prepare thoroughly for your own exam this summer.

Be aware that as of 2003 English and Communication is now simply called English. The exam consists of two papers: Close Reading and Critical Essay; you will no longer be examined on unseen textual analysis in the examination. Nevertheless, all past papers in this book, including the newly formatted 2003 exam, will still assess your subject appreciation and also your ability to apply examinable skills developed throughout the course.

By referring to the answer booklet you will understand exactly what the examiner is looking for to gain a top mark and will be able to focus on and improve in particular areas of your course which you find difficult. Remember too to use the top tips for revision and sitting the exam to make sure you perform to the best of your ability.

Practice makes perfect. Use these past papers to make sure you know what to expect on the day and are ready to succeed.

Good luck!

Acknowledgements

Every effort has been made to trace the copyright holders and to obtain their permission for the use of copyright material. Leckie & Leckie will gladly receive information enabling them to rectify any error or omission in subsequent editions.

Faber & Faber for the poem 'Blackberry Picking' from *Death of a Naturalist* by Seamus Heaney (1999 SQP Paper II p 2) and an extract from *Oscar and Lucinda* by Peter Carey (2000 Analysis and Appreciation p 2);
Sam Toperoff for the article *Tarantula* (2000 Interpretation p 2);
Jimmy Glen for the short story *The Vase* (2001 Analysis and Appreciation p 2);
Brian McCabe for the poem *Rat* (2002 Analysis and Appreciation p 2);
An extract from *For Love and Money* by Jonathan Raban published by Harvill. Reprinted by permission of The Random House Group Ltd. (2003 Close Reading p 2).

The following companies have very generously given permission to reproduce their copyright material free of charge:
'Trainer Spotting: The Sport of the Nineties' by Alison Thomas. Reproduced with the permission of *The Herald/Evening Times* (1999 SQP Paper I p 2);
The Sunday Herald for an extract from the article 'Manhattan Transfer' by Aaron Hinklen (2001 Close Reading p 2);
Extract from *A Walk in the Woods* by Bill Bryson, published by Black Swan, a division of Transworld Publishers. © Bill Bryson. All rights reserved. (2002 Close Reading p 2);
Brian Millar for the article *How To Make Science Lovable* (2003 SQP Close Reading p 2).

INTERMEDIATE 2 1999 SQP

[C039/SQP071]

Intermediate 2 Time: 1 hour
English
Paper I: Interpretation
Specimen Question Paper

NATIONAL
QUALIFICATIONS

You should attempt all questions.

The total value of the Paper is 40 marks.

SCOTTISH
QUALIFICATIONS
AUTHORITY

The passage that follows is a newspaper article about the popularity of certain types of sports shoe.

Read the passage carefully and then answer all the questions, using your own words as far as possible.

The questions on it will ask you to show that:

> you understand the main ideas and important details in the passage—in other words, **what** the writer has said (**Understanding—U**);
>
> you can identify, using appropriate terms, the techniques the writer has used to get across these ideas—in other words, **how** she has said it (**Analysis—A**);
>
> you can, using appropriate evidence, comment on how effective the writer has been—in other words **how well** she has said it (**Evaluation—E**).
>
> A code letter, (U : A : E) is used alongside each question to identify its purpose for you.

Trainer Spotting : the Sport of The Nineties

Alison Thomas rues the day sports shoe manufacturers put the boot into family budgets by going hi-tech.

IT'S an all-too-familiar scenario to parents across the country. Weeks of alternate wheedling and sulking concluding in a compromise that pleases no-one—a pair of trainers that cost a lot more than you'd bargained for, but can't compare with the latest hi-tech model your fashion-conscious teenager coveted.

Hostilities die down for a few days, only to flare up again when you receive a frosty letter from school reminding you of your parental duty to support their policy on uniform. Having effected a surreptitious switch of footwear at the bus-stop, your insubordinate offspring has been spotted by the headmistress.

Even the French, who find our attitude to uniform rather quaint, if not positively eccentric, are trying to dissuade young people from wearing trainers to school. As the headteacher of one school in Bergerac put it "If you allow trainers, pupils will wear the same shoes all day long, including sports lessons. You can imagine the result—the classroom smells like a farmyard!"

The origins of high technology footwear go back to the Mexico Olympics in 1968 when tartan athletics tracks were introduced for the first time. Fourteen world records fell that year, and the trend continued as more and more stadiums adopted the new surface. But there was a price to pay. Athletes weren't used to competing on hard surfaces, and before long doctors noticed a marked increase in the number of injuries such as Achilles tendon and cartilage problems. They nicknamed it the "tartan syndrome".

However, it wasn't until 1977 that a Swiss researcher identified the cause of the problem, a discovery which led to a revolution in shoe manufacturing techniques. When an athlete is running on a hard surface, his spinal column shudders each time his foot hits the ground. Even a gentle jog can produce an impact three times his body weight. Ever since, manufacturers have spent millions of pounds developing new ways of cushioning the force of this impact, until today some of them claim reductions of up to 52%.

Yet most of the teenagers who buy top-of-the-range hi-tech trainers rarely go near a sports track. So why is it that wearing the latest model is so important if you value your street cred?

The French word for trainer is "basket", short for basketball, and this is where it all started—on the basketball court. In America, basketball stars are cult figures, especially among ethnic minority groups, for this sport is one of the few avenues open to young blacks aspiring to climb the social ladder. From there it spread to other young people, and, as with most American trends, it wasn't long before the latest craze had crossed the Atlantic.

Today, the giants of the sports shoe industry are engaged in a cut-throat battle to cling on to their share of the market. Their weapons are a plethora of new models, each one more technologically advanced than the one before, and vast sums spent on advertising and marketing.

Basketball heroes Shaquille O'Neale and Michael Jordan, football idols Ryan Giggs and Ian Wright, star athletes Daley Thompson and Linford Christie—all of these have lent their names to leading models, ensuring that to wear any other make is "totally sad". The music world too exerts its influence. Adidas were lagging behind until the "Gazelle", worn by Madonna and other female vocalists, became all the rage with young girls. They're not as hi-tech as Nike or Reebok, but they're cheaper, and they're just the thing for an evening out.

Bemused parents watch their daughters spend hours perfecting a sophisticated appearance only to cap it all—or foot it all—with this low cut, striped shoe reminiscent of the 1970s.

You might be forgiven for concluding that it's all one enormous marketing gimmick and a total

waste of your money. Sophisticated cushion soles may be essential for the stars of the sporting world, but they're pretty irrelevant for your average
85 sedentary teenager. Yet that's the rub. For in some ways, modern trainers are actually good for their feet, especially if they spend most of their time loafing around the town centre or hanging out with their mates on street corners.

90 For the less fit you are, the more your tendons and cartilages are susceptible to damage. Even embarrassingly out-of-touch parents could do worse than give them a try. A good shock absorber can be an asset if you're overweight, suffer from
95 back problems or walk a lot on hard surfaces like pavements.

But trainers do have one drawback—they're not good at absorbing moisture. A recent survey examining the sweat absorption capacity of
100 13 models concluded that four were "inadequate", the other nine "very inadequate". In view of this, coupled with the fact that an hour's exercise produces 15–20 grams of sweat, it's not surprising that before long our children's feet are squelching pungently inside their shoes. And what is 105 particularly worrying is to see so many 16–18 year olds wearing the same pair of shoes day in day out all year long.

Which brings us back to the aroma lingering in Bergerac classrooms. The saga of the dissident 110 young Nicholas of year 10, who was sent home for insisting on wearing his trainers to school, caused quite a furore. Although the headteacher managed to persuade the school's administrative council to back him, he then had to face the parents' 115 association, who lodged a formal appeal against the trainer ban. But then the French are rather quaint, if not positively eccentric.

QUESTIONS

		Marks	Code

1. In the first two paragraphs (lines 1–14), what techniques has the writer used to get **the reader** involved in the article?   **2 A**

2. Clearly explain the compromise described in paragraph 1.   **2 U**

3. How had the "offspring" referred to in line 13 been "insubordinate"?   **2 U**

4. (a) What does the writer gain by opening the third paragraph (line 15) with the word "Even"?   **2 A**

    (b) **In your own words**, what appears to be the **usual** attitude of the French towards the clothes people wear to school?   **1 U**

    (c) Why do they take a different attitude towards wearing trainers?   **1 U**

5. (a) **Using your own words as far as possible**, outline the development of hi-tech footwear as conveyed in lines 23–44.   **3 U**

    (b) In what way could the present popularity of such footwear be regarded as ironic?   **2 U**

    (c) "So why is it that wearing the latest model is so important if you value your street cred?" (lines 47–48)
       In your own words, what answers does the writer provide to this question in lines 49–75?   **3 U**

6. **Look at the fourth paragraph** (lines 23–33).
   Think about the way this paragraph is organised.
   What aspects of **the structure** of the paragraph help the writer to convey her meaning effectively?   **3 U**

7. Give an example and explain how the writer's **choice of words** in lines 58–63 emphasises the **nature** of the competition between the companies producing trainers.   **3 A**

8. What is the **main advantage** and what is the **main disadvantage** of wearing hi-tech trainers even if you do not take part in sport?   **2 U**

9. How effective is the final paragraph?
   Use evidence from the article to support your view.   **2 E**

Marks Code

10. (a) The writer uses **humour** throughout this article.
Select an example from lines 76–118 and explain why it is effective. 2 E

(b) Select **two** of the following and explain how they help her to achieve her purpose:

the use of illustration;

the tone employed;

the use of figurative language;

word choice;

structure.

Support your comments with direct evidence from the text. 6 E

11. Look again at the by-line used by the editor to introduce this article, "*Alison . . . going hi-tech.*"

Referring directly to words or phrases used in this by-line, explain to what extent you believe it **is** or **is not** an accurate reflection of the passage. 4 E

Total (40)

[END OF QUESTION PAPER]

[C039/SQP071]

Intermediate 2 Time: 1 hour 30 minutes **NATIONAL QUALIFICATIONS**
English
Paper II
Specimen Question Paper

This paper consists of two parts: Part(a)—Textual Analysis
                                    Part(b)—Critical Essay

You should attempt all questions in the Textual Analysis part of the Paper. The value of this part is 30 marks.

You should attempt only **one** question from the Critical Essay part of the Paper. The value of this part is 30 marks.

PART (a)—TEXTUAL ANALYSIS

Read this poem about picking blackberries (brambles) and answer the questions which follow.

The questions are in two sections.

The questions in the Analysis section ask you about **what** the poet has said and **how** he has said it.

The questions in the Appreciation section ask you to give your personal reaction to the poem, commenting on how effective you found the techniques used by the poet and providing evidence from the poem to justify your reactions.

BLACKBERRY PICKING

Late August, given heavy rain and sun
For a full week, the blackberries would ripen.
At first, just one, a glossy purple clot
Among others, red, green, hard as a knot.
5 You ate that first one and its flesh was sweet
Like thickened wine: summer's blood was in it
Leaving stains upon the tongue and lust for
Picking. Then red ones inked up and that hunger
Sent us out with milk-cans, pea-tins, jam-pots
10 Where briars scratched and wet grass bleached our boots.
Round hayfields, cornfields and potato-drills
We trekked and picked until the cans were full,
Until the tinkling bottom had been covered
With green ones, and on top big dark blobs burned
15 Like a plate of eyes. Our hands were peppered
With thorn pricks, our palms sticky as Bluebeard's*

We hoarded the fresh berries in the byre
But when the bath was filled we found a fur,
A rat-grey fungus, glutting on our cache.
20 The juice was stinking too. Once off the bush
The fruit fermented, the sweet flesh would turn sour.
I always felt like crying. It wasn't fair
That all the lovely canfuls smelt of rot.
Each year I hoped they'd keep, knew they would not.

Seamus Heaney

*Bluebeard was a folk tale villain famous for murdering his wives.

QUESTIONS

Analysis

Marks

1. Why is the poem divided into two sections?
   Your answer should deal briefly with the content of each section. **3**

2. In lines 2–8 the poet illustrates the difference between the ripe and the unripe berries.
   Quoting at least **two** examples show how the poet's choice of imagery makes this difference clear. **4**

3. Explain how any **two** of the following words help to recreate a child's experience of picking blackberries (brambles):
   "trekked" (line 12)
   "tinkling" (line 13)
   "peppered" (line 15) **4**

4. Look at lines 14–16.
   How do the images contained in these lines suggest a sense of wrongdoing? **4**

5. By close reference to any two poetic techniques used in lines 18–21 (such as word-choice, imagery, sound, structure . . .), show how the poet reinforces the impression of decay. **4**

Appreciation

6. (a) In the last three lines of the poem the narration changes from first person plural to first person singular.
   What effect does this change have on you as a reader of the poem? **1**

   (b) In what other ways are the last three lines (22–24) an effective conclusion to the poem?
   You should refer both to content and to poetic techniques. **4**

7. Referring to those features of the poem which impressed you most, show how the poet uses a childhood experience to comment on human nature. **6**

Total (30)

[END OF PART (a)—TEXTUAL ANALYSIS]

PART (b)—CRITICAL ESSAY

You should attempt **one** question only, taken from any section. Write the number of the question you attempt in the margin of your answer book.

DRAMA

1. Choose a play which explores an issue of a social, political or religious nature.

    How does the playwright present the play in such a way as to convince you of the importance of the issue?

    In your answer you must refer to the text and to at least **two** of: theme, characterisation, staging, outcome, key scene(s).

2. Choose a play in which the relationship between two main characters either improves, or deteriorates.

    Trace the change in the relationship and show what effect this has on the events and on the other characters in the play.

    In your answer you must refer to the text and to at least **two** of: plot, characterisation, key scene(s), dialogue, conflict.

3. Choose a scene which forms the climax of a play.

    Briefly describe the events of the scene, and then go on to show to what extent the scene you have described seems to you to be important in dictating the final events of the play.

    In your answer you must refer closely to the text and to at least **two** of: structure, plot, characterisation, outcome.

PROSE

4. Choose a novel (or short story) in which a main character becomes steadily more isolated.

    How does the increasing isolation affect the character's attitudes, actions and self-knowledge and your sympathies for him/her?

    In your answer you must refer closely to the text and to at least **two** of: characterisation, theme, plot, narrative stance.

5. A short story often ends in a surprising but satisfying way.

    Concentrating on the ending of a story, explain the success of the ending for you.

    In your answer you must refer closely to the text and to at least **two** of: structure, plot, conflict, characterisation.

6. Choose a novel or a non-fiction book dealing with travel where the sense of place and/or people created is an important element.

    Show how, in your opinion, this element of the book is central to your appreciation of the ideas or themes of the book.

    In your answer you must refer closely to the text and to at least **two** of: setting, characterisation, quality of writing, theme.

POETRY

7. Choose a poem which starts with a description of an everyday event or incident, but which then explores more serious issues.

    Discuss how effectively the poet uses the initial particular incident to lead to a general or universal statement.

    In your answer you must refer closely to the text and to at least **two** of: theme, structure, word-choice, imagery.

8. Choose a poem in which a particular mood such as joy, anger, sorrow is created.

    State what the mood is and show how the poet has created it effectively for you.

    In your answer you must refer closely to the text and to at least **two** of: imagery, word-choice, tone, sound.

9. Choose a poem which successfully describes a place, **or** a person, **or** an animal.

    Show how the important features of the subject of the poem are illustrated in such a way as to make an impact on you.

    In your answer you must refer closely to the text and to at least **two** of: word-choice, imagery, characterisation, setting.

MASS MEDIA

10. Choose a film or television drama which contains a sequence of great excitement or tension.

    Briefly explain the context of the sequence you have chosen in the film or drama as a whole and go on to show how the excitement or tension you feel is created.

    In your answer you must refer closely to the text and to at least **two** of: use of camera, soundtrack, editing, conflict.

11. Family life is the subject of many television dramas, serials, or series. Choose a suitable drama of this type.

    Show how relationships within a family are portrayed in a way which catches your interest.

    In your answer you must refer closely to the text and to at least **two** of: genre, characterisation, casting, dialogue, clothing.

12. Choose a commercially successful film which is set in Scotland.

    What factors, do you think, contributed to its success?

    In your answer you must refer closely to the text and to at least **two** of: setting, use of stars, theme, clothing, use of camera, editing.

[END OF QUESTION PAPER]

[BLANK PAGE]

INTERMEDIATE 2 2000

X039/201

NATIONAL
QUALIFICATIONS
2000

WEDNESDAY, 24 MAY
9.00 AM – 10.00 AM

ENGLISH AND
COMMUNICATION
INTERMEDIATE 2
Interpretation

You should attempt all questions.

The total value of the Paper is 40 marks.

The passage which follows is adapted from an article that appeared in a magazine entitled "Beasts".

Read the passage carefully and then answer **all** the questions, **using your own words as far as possible**.

The questions will ask you to show that:

> you understand the main ideas and important details in the passage—in other words, **what** the writer has said (**Understanding—U**);
>
> you can identify, using appropriate terms, the techniques the writer has used to get across these ideas—in other words, **how** he has said it (**Analysis—A**);
>
> you can, using appropriate evidence, comment on how effective the writer has been—in other words **how well** he has said it (**Evaluation—E**).

A code letter (U, A, E) is used alongside each question to identify its purpose for you. The number of marks attached to each question will give some indication of the length of answer required.

TARANTULA

Sam Toperoff attempts to improve the image of a notorious species of spider.

I'm nocturnal. I love the moonlight, the shadows, the dark places, the dappled murk. I'm not being poetic. I'm simply being true to my nature, my nocturnal nature. Like all tarantulas.

5 At the moment I'm in El Capitan, the only old-time theatre left in downtown Amarillo, West Texas.

I know the place well. Usually I saunter in under the Ladies' Room door a little after dark, find my 10 armrest along the wall, watch the feature, get a little hungry, and vamoose. Sometimes I don't even have to leave the theatre to find something tasty: an oversized cockroach or a kid mouse. There's nothing like a good snack when you're 15 watching a movie.

I guess you can tell that behind my rough exterior I'm really a romantic kind of guy at heart. That's a line from *Wolf*, in case you don't know. Jack Nicholson. I love Jack. People say I look like 20 him.

Anyway, I'm here watching *Kilimanjaro*, which I thought would be garbage, mostly because of all the hype about it and the fact that it came in about a billion dollars over budget. It's the remake, 25 with Tom Cruise and Nicole Kidman.

I don't see real well. None of us do. If I squint, it's fine; fuzzy, but fine. And the music, unbelievable. One of those giant speakers is only a couple of rows up front. When the bass fiddles and the timpani 30 come in, I vibrate. Every single cilia quivers. Maybe it's the music more than anything that draws me in. And the credits: the way the credits crawl up the screen is really a turn on. It makes me dizzy, in a mellow way.

35 Did I tell you I've been here three days now, or what I take to be three days? It's hard to tell when it stays dark like it does in here. Usually, every time the theatre empties after the last show, I know that it's time to leave. But at the moment I can't get out.

They've boarded up the Ladies' Room. Repairs. 40 Think what it means to be nocturnal and stuck in a movie theatre. Eternal nocturnal—too much of a good thing. I can't even sleep, though I am tired beyond belief.

So I'm watching *Kilimanjaro*. Seen it, seen it, and 45 seen it. And let me tell you: no Oscars for this baby. Except there's this one scene. Maybe you remember it. It's the one where Tom Cruise, the great white hunter, goes into Nicole's tent at night with his lantern. He's sneaking around but doesn't 50 want it to look that way—and that speaks to me; I also hate to look like I'm skulking. Anyway, it's really hokey but I love it. I know. I'm a hopeless romantic.

So when he gets inside her tent she's sleeping, or 55 pretending to be sleeping, underneath this mosquito netting. I think you can see her eyelashes flutter, but can't be absolutely sure. She's wearing a lacy nightgown, pink. On safari, a pink nightie? Tom watches. 60

She moves and makes a little sound, a sigh, still sleeping. Her hand slides up the pillow. And there—right there—coming down the pillow sideways is a black fist. The first time, I couldn't believe it. It was one of us—one of me. A young, 65 really good-looking tarantula.

He moves elegantly, to the pizzicato strings of the Hollywood Bowl Orchestra. Two, two-and-a-half inches long. Tall, remarkably regular features, narrow white fangs, nice smile, sort of shy. You 70 can see how he got the part. So he comes down the pillow—the violins stop—and steps on to her shoulder. How he lifts and curls his front legs. It's so graceful.

And they never see it. The audience. They don't 75 see the grace, the elegance. They see . . . I

know what they see. Usually they are disgusted, revolted, repelled, nauseated—any word of loathing you want to use. They don't even notice
80 his lovely smile.

Why do they hate us? We have fangs, sure, and venom. But we do not—let me repeat: not—attack human beings. Certainly not a sleeping innocent— relatively speaking—like Nicole Kidman. Yet
85 there's this attitude: Tarantula equals terror. Like it was one of us back there in the Garden of Eden or something.

In Europe—especially in Italy—they still believe that a tarantula bite can be fatal. But tell me, why
90 would we want to poison anything we weren't going to eat? In order to ward off death, they think, you have to dance like a dervish. The Tarantella. They whirl, they jump, they bounce, to fight off the lethargy, the paralysis. What can I tell you—
95 people. Once, they even believed that a bite was communicable, so whole towns would dance for hours and hours, until the last dancer fell exhausted to the ground, bathed in sweat. When the last dancer goes down, the town is cured,
100 apparently. I'd love to see something like that in Amarillo. Want the truth? A man could hold us in the palm of his hand, and we'd never bite him. How'd you think they trained that guy for *Kilimanjaro*? And even if by some wild chance we
105 did bite someone, what would it be like? No worse than a hornet's sting. And are they despised, as we are? Well, maybe, but loathed? I don't think so.

It's simple: if we're hungry, we eat—just like you. In *Kilimanjaro*, when the safari needed dinner
110 they killed a wildebeest, and Tom had the locals roast it on a spit. No problem. But when I stun and numb a mouse, eat it in morsels, ingest it and leave the skin and skeleton, I'm disgusting. Come on.

I'm nine years old—early middle age; we live into
115 our twenties. Mom laid 200 eggs. I didn't hang around, and neither did any of my brothers and sisters. I left the cocoon for a dark, peaceful burrow as soon as I could form this thought: *leave the cocoon for a dark, peaceful burrow.*

120 As I already mentioned, we don't see or hear too well. But these faculties are not really necessary because, well, I'm tactile. Every living thing is tactile, but not Tarantula-tactile. We are to touch what an eagle is to sight. Brush my body wall in
125 even the slightest way and I'll know almost everything about you. Believe me. Usually, I'll zip away, unless I'm hungry, in which case I might grab at whatever's tickling. And every once in a while, if I don't want to be bothered, I'll lean back,
130 raise my front legs like Bruce Lee, and bare my fangs. It's a ferocious pose. It usually does the job.

It's the fine hairs—setae, cilia, call them what you will—that warn me of danger. They cover my entire body. Dark, dark hairs. My friend Nathan
135 tells me he's seen a film at the university where a cricket barely touches the body fuzz of a tarantula. The spider attacks, and even slowed to one sixty-fourth of a second you can't see the strike. You see only a blur, and then a dead cricket. I'd love to see
140 that film. It's rare to see us in a starring role.

In Turkey, Nathan tells me, people use us to catch flies. I've always imagined an evening in Istanbul: tarantulas bouncing around a million bedroom walls like black tennis balls. Flies disappearing—
145 thrrrippp, thrrrippp, thrrrippp. Advantage Tarantula.

I'm not your run-of-the-mill specimen. Certainly, when my *trichobothria*—the especially sensitive hair on my legs—is riffled, I want to kill. I say
150 "want", but it's not a want: it's a—what's the word? There is no word exactly, it's just a Tarantula thing, and I can't control it. I just . . . But I can control lots of other things. That's why I'm not your run-of-the-mill. I don't know if it's a
155 good thing to go against your deepest nature, but I've been doing it. I have an enquiring mind. I want to be, well, a little less Tarantula in some ways. Maybe it's because I can afford to be. I'm large and powerful. And it's like Nicholson said in *The Shining*: it's nice not to have to be afraid—
160 gives a man plenty of slack. Then again, maybe I've seen too many movies.

Adapted from an article by *Sam Toperoff*

Official SQA Past Papers: Intermediate 2 English 2000

QUESTIONS

Marks Code

1. The writer writes this article as if he were a tarantula talking to us.

    Quoting evidence from the early part of the passage (lines 1–20), show how the writer creates the impression of someone **speaking to us** rather than writing for us.   2 A

2. (a) **In your own words**, in what way is the speaker "like all tarantulas" according to the first paragraph?   1 U

    (b) What disadvantages is this characteristic said to have **later** in the passage?   2 U

    (c) Write down **two** other things we learn about the speaker from lines 5–34 that are likely to be true of all tarantulas.   2 U

3. Quote an expression from the first three paragraphs (lines 1–15) that suggests that the speaker does not feel threatened in the film theatre.   1 A

4. In the first part of the article (lines 1–74), the tarantula is presented as a film fan.

    In what ways is he a keen film fan?   2 U

5. Look at lines 45–74.

    (a) What is the speaker's opinion of the film *Kilimanjaro* and how does he make this clear?   2 A

    (b) Quote the expression that makes it clear that he identifies with the actions of the Tom Cruise character in the film.   1 A

    (c) How does he convey his surprise at seeing one of his own kind "starring" in a film?   1 A

    (d) "You can see how he got the part." (lines 70–71)
    What quality gained this "star" the part, according to the speaker?   1 U

6. At line 75, the mood of the speaker seems to change.

    (a) In what way does it change?   2 U

    (b) How do the structure **and** word choice of lines 75–80 reinforce this change?   4 A

7. (a) With what creature do humans equate the tarantula, according to lines 81–87?   1 U

    (b) In your own words, what **two** physical features do tarantulas have in common with this creature?   2 U

8. The speaker provides several pieces of evidence to support his argument that the fear of tarantulas is unjustified.

    Summarise the main ones given in lines 88–113.   3 U

9. (a) What asset compensates for the tarantula's poor sight and hearing?   1 U

    (b) Select **one** expression used to describe this asset and explain why you find it effective.   2 A

10. Giving reasons for your answer, explain how effectively you think lines 147–162 **round off** the article.   4 E

11. The editorial comment introducing the passage suggests that the writer's purpose is to "improve the image" of the tarantula.

    Giving examples to support your answer, explain how the writer has used **any three** of the following features to help him improve the tarantula's image:

    - figures of speech
    - word choice, including the use of technical terms
    - structure and/or word order
    - techniques of argument such as illustration, comparison, contrast, proof and disproof
    - the style, tone or register adopted
    - humour.   6 E

    Total (40)

[*END OF QUESTION PAPER*]

X039/202

NATIONAL QUALIFICATIONS 2000

WEDNESDAY, 24 MAY 10.20 AM — 11.50 AM

ENGLISH AND COMUNICATION INTERMEDIATE 2
Analysis and Appreciation

There are **two parts** to this paper and you should attempt both parts.

Part 1 (Textual Analysis) is worth 30 marks.

In Part 2 (Critical Essay), you should attempt **one** question only, taken from any of the Sections A–D.

Your answer to Part 2 should begin on a fresh page.

Each question in Part 2 is worth 30 marks.

NB You must not use, in Part 2 of this paper, the same text(s) as you have used in your Specialist Study.

PART 1—TEXTUAL ANALYSIS

Read the following extract from a novel and answer the questions which follow.

You are reminded that this part of the paper tests your ability to understand, analyse and evaluate the text.

The number of marks attached to each question will give some indication of the length of answer required.

You should spend about 45 minutes on this part of the paper.

OSCAR AND LUCINDA

Lucinda is an eighteen-year-old woman who has inherited a large sum of money. She has left Parramatta, the small town in Australia where she has been living, to travel to Sydney, looking for opportunities to invest in a business. She enters Sydney harbour on a boat captained by Sol Myer. The date is about 1860.

They passed the jumbled mud-smeared logs of Walter O'Brien's Colonial Timber Mill just as the sun dropped beneath Pyrmont. They passed beneath the peeling walls of MacArthur's Flour Mill: it was a grey weatherboard structure, tall and thin and leaning sideways at an angle.

The waterfront seemed clogged with logs, iron, sheets of corrugated roofing, abused timber with giant bolts rusting in it. Lucinda was afraid. She felt very small. She wished Sol Myer would suddenly demand that she act her age and return to Parramatta.

Her arms, beneath her cape, were goose-pimpling. She wound a cotton scarf around her face and blew into her hands. Sol swung the wheel and, as the boat came about, she saw these words: Prince Rupert's Glassworks. The board that bore the words was weathered and faded—lime green against a poison blue.

10 The works were all in shadow, like a stranger's face under a hat, and not any more inviting because of it. You could not see what it was, how it was made, how it was put together. There were sheds, a chimney with black smoke. It could have been a blacksmith's, were it not for the crates of bottles.

These glassworks were for sale. There was a sign that said so, not a new sign, but more recent than the one that said Prince Rupert's. They looked intimidating, almost evil. Very well, she thought, if that is what it is to be.
15 She made this decision without understanding that there existed, within this city, places with trees and grass and flowers.

Sol brought his craft into the wharf, sliding it gently through the smaller craft, like a careful hand amongst bobbing apples. Lucinda stood up. The crinoline cage* swayed. She moved along the edge of the boat self-consciously. She felt all the wharf was looking at her, but she was wrong. She took her own case down from
20 the cabin roof. It was heavy with books. The case banged against her thigh and bruised it. She did not know anything about Sydney. She did not know how to engage an omnibus or a hansom cab, what they cost, where they went or how they were stopped. She paid Mr Myer sixpence for the journey. He gave her a cauliflower and then, in a bristly rush, a kiss on her cold cheek. He delivered her on to the wharf amongst hessian bags and steel-wheeled trolleys. She struggled up the hill from the wharf with her suitcase banging against her right
25 side, a cauliflower clutched in her left hand. The suitcase put her skirt cage violently off centre. This is how she arrived at Petty's Hotel. At first they thought her at the wrong address. She placed her cauliflower on the desk and asked them, blushing brightly, if there was a reliable library close to the hotel.

She had decided to study glass.

Peter Carey

*A hooped underskirt worn in Victorian times.

QUESTIONS

Marks

1. Look at lines 1–3.

    (a) An unpleasant impression of Sydney harbour is given in this paragraph. How is this impression created? You should refer closely to the text in your answer. **2**

    (b) How does the sentence structure of this paragraph help to reinforce the idea of time passing on Lucinda's journey through the harbour? **2**

2. How does the sentence structure of lines 4–5 emphasise Lucinda's feelings on entering the harbour? **2**

3. Lines 8–14 describe Prince Rupert's Glassworks.

    (a) What impression does the simile in line 10 give of the glassworks? **1**

    (b) Explain how it does so. **1**

    (c) By selecting any **two** other single words from lines 8–14, show how this impression is reinforced. **3**

4. (a) How is Sol Myer's skill emphasised in lines 17–18? **2**

    (b) Refer to two of Sol's actions in lines 22–24 and suggest what each reveals about his personality. You should refer to the text in support of your answer. **4**

5. Look at lines 24–27.

    Give **two** reasons why the staff of Petty's Hotel might think that she had got the wrong address. **2**

6. In the last line we are told: "She had decided to study glass."

    What decision did she make in line 14? You should justify your answer by reference to information you are given in the introduction to the extract and to the information you are given in lines 13–16 and in the last line. **3**

7. One of the main functions of this extract is to expand the reader's knowledge of Lucinda's personality and characteristics.

    (a) How successful do you think the writer has been in conveying Lucinda's inexperience and self-consciousness in lines 17–28? You should support your answer by close reference to the text. **4**

    (b) Looking at the passage as a whole, identify two other aspects of Lucinda's personality which are revealed through her actions. Show how they add to your overall impression of her. You should refer closely to the passage in your answer. **4**

Total **(30)**

[Turn over for PART 2—CRITICAL ESSAY

PART 2—CRITICAL ESSAY

Attempt ONE question only, taken from any of the Sections A to D. Write the number of the question you attempt in the margin of your answer book.

In all Sections you may use Scottish texts.

You must not use the extract from the Textual Analysis part of the paper as the subject of your Critical Essay.

You are reminded that the quality of your writing and its accuracy are important in this paper as is the relevance of your answer to the question you have attempted.

You should spend about 45 minutes on this part of the paper.

Begin your answer on a fresh page.

SECTION A—DRAMA

1. Choose a play in which an important character is in conflict with another character or characters in the play, or with herself or himself.

    Describe the conflict and show in what way it is important to the development of the plot and theme of the play.

    In your answer you must refer to the text and to at least **two** of: theme, plot, characterisation, climax or any other appropriate feature.

2. Choose a play which deals with family life.

    How are the relationships between members of the family portrayed and to what extent do you find these relationships convincing?

    In your answer you must refer to the text and to at least **two** of: characterisation, key scene(s), conflict, dialogue or any other appropriate feature.

3. Choose a play which seems to you to have a memorable opening scene or section.

    Show how the scene or section is effective in giving you important information about one, or more than one, of the following: characters; situation; mood of the play.

    In your answer you must refer to the text and to at least **two** of: structure, characterisation, dialogue, setting, tone or any other appropriate feature.

SECTION B—PROSE

4. Choose a novel or short story in which you feel great sympathy for, or intense dislike of, one of the characters.

    Briefly outline the situation in which the character finds himself or herself and show by what means you are made to feel sympathy or dislike.

    In your answer you must refer closely to the text and to at least **two** of: characterisation, setting, climax, narrative, technique or any other appropriate feature.

5. Choose a prose work of fiction or non-fiction which deals with an important human issue: for example injustice, or poverty, or scientific discovery, or religious belief, or any other issue which you regard as important.

    Identify and explain what the issue is and go on to describe the ways in which the writer has made the prose work thought-provoking.

    In your answer you must refer closely to the text and to at least **two** of: theme, language, narrative stance, tone, setting or any other appropriate feature.

6. Choose a short story which has humorous aspects—perhaps character or situation or use of language, or the ending.

    Describe what you feel to be the humorous aspect(s) of the story and go on to show how the aspect(s) affected your appreciation of the short story.

    In your answer you must refer closely to the text and to at least **two** of: characterisation, language, dialogue, structure or any other appropriate feature.

SECTION C—POETRY

7. Choose a poem which recreates for you a feeling or emotion which you have experienced.

   Explain how the poem, by its content and style, does this.

   In your answer you must refer closely to the text and to at least **two** of: mood, word-choice, imagery, sound or any other appropriate feature.

8. Choose a poem which tells the story of an event or a character or an incident.

   Briefly outline the story and go on to say what techniques are used in the poem to catch and maintain your interest.

   In your answer you must refer closely to the text and to at least **two** of: word-choice, imagery, structure, characterisation, rhythm or any other appropriate feature.

9. Choose a poem which deals with an aspect of the less pleasant side of life.

   Show how the poem increases your knowledge and understanding of the aspect of life dealt with, and how the use of poetic technique contributes to the impact the poem had on you.

   In your answer you must refer closely to the text and to at least **two** of: word-choice, imagery, tone or any other appropriate feature.

SECTION D—MASS MEDIA

10. Choose a film or TV drama or serial which is set in a past age.

    Show how the director has fully recreated the setting of the period and discuss how this aspect of the film/drama/serial adds to your enjoyment.

    In your answer you must refer closely to the text and to at least **two** of: setting, costume, dialogue, mood, use of camera or any other appropriate feature.

11. Choose a film in which there is a great deal of fast and exciting action.

    By selecting appropriate scenes from the film, show how the fast action is important in arousing and maintaining your interest in the film.

    In your answer you must refer closely to the text and to at least **two** of: editing, sound track, use of camera, special effects or any other appropriate feature.

12. TV dramas, series or serials often both entertain and help raise awareness of social issues.

    With reference to one such drama, series or serial explain how these two aspects are successfully combined.

    In your answer you must refer closely to the text and to at least **two** of: theme, setting, use of stars, dialogue or any other appropriate feature.

[END OF QUESTION PAPER]

[BLANK PAGE]

INTERMEDIATE 2 2001

X039/201

| NATIONAL QUALIFICATIONS 2001 | TUESDAY, 15 MAY 9.00 AM – 10.00 AM | ENGLISH AND COMMUNICATION INTERMEDIATE 2 Close Reading |

You should attempt all questions.

The total value of the Paper is 30 marks.

The passage which follows is adapted from the Travel section of a newspaper.

Read the passage carefully and then answer **all** the questions, **using your own words as far as possible**.

The questions will ask you to show that:

> you understand the main ideas and important details in the passage—in other words, **what** the writer has said (**Understanding—U**);
>
> you can identify, using appropriate terms, the techniques the writer has used to get across these ideas—in other words, **how** he has said it (**Analysis—A**);
>
> you can, using appropriate evidence, comment on how effective the writer has been—in other words **how well** he has said it (**Evaluation—E**).

A code letter (U, A, E) is used alongside each question to identify its purpose for you. The number of marks attached to each question will give some indication of the length of answer required.

Taxi!

Aaron Hinklin remembers a New York cabby.

Tourists are always wanting to jump in cabs, as if the fact they are yellow and look just like they do on TV gives it some kind of meaning, but every New Yorker hates them with a vengeance. They are designed to remind you that life is a fragile commodity and that, at any moment, you might lose yours. They are cramped, airless death traps and
5 they come equipped with the drivers they deserve. They are the kind of drivers that are imported for the purpose of scaring you witless. It works.

Under other circumstances, I would have taken the subway. Even though everyone knows that the subway will be the first target of terrorists, it's still safer than taking a cab. But I'd been shopping at Balducci's, my favourite New York deli, and was loath to
10 manoeuvre my bags into the crowded, subterranean world where the sun never shone.

Outside it felt like summer, whereas the subway knows no season. I wanted to cruise over the Brooklyn Bridge and gaze at the Statue of Liberty and pick at my fresh California strawberries.

The moment I stepped into the taxi I knew something was wrong. For a start the driver
15 was called Eddie and taxi drivers in New York shouldn't have names. They should be anonymous, for then you can be rude and condescending to them without guilt.

Eddie would not allow me to be rude and condescending, even though I did my usual grumbling act. I could see him glaring in his mirror. It was the kind of glare I've come to know well, a glare that says: "I am only tolerating this arrogant guy because he is my
20 passenger and because I am accustomed to rude, arrogant passengers." But it turned out I was wrong, because then he began talking, which was not part of the deal.

It turned out that Eddie was not Eddie after all, but a rock star named Joe Betts. At least, this was the alternative reality he had created for himself.

Joe Betts was born in Queens, grew up in Brooklyn and was almost discovered at the
25 1964 World Fair in New York at which he came second in the Battle of the Bands. He played Café Wah in McDougal Street with some guy who would later end up in The New York Dolls. He was 16 and he was going to be a rock star.

Joe didn't mind that he ended up driving cabs instead. The cab was going to make him famous. It was thanks to the cab that he'd made a video with Joe Pesci and Robert De
30 Niro, well, okay, not *the* Joe Pesci and Robert De Niro, but a pair of lookalikes.

He had also done Lenny Bruce for a Swatch commercial, well, okay, not a *Swatch* commercial but some in-house video that got canned. And then there was the feature in New York magazine. Well, okay, not *really* about him but he was mentioned. They called him The Last American Cab Driver. Had I read it? As it happened I hadn't,
35 which was hardly surprising since it appeared in December 1997. But time was inconsequential to Joe, just as driving a cab was incidental. It was a means to an end. It would make him famous. A publisher from St Martin's Press once jumped into the back of his cab and offered him a deal. That was two years ago. Joe is still working on the title.

40 Thirty years of incidentally driving a cab is a long time but Joe was convinced that his moment would come. He didn't seem to recognise the sadness in these things as I did. For me, it seemed his story illuminated thwarted ambition and the inevitable compromise between the aims of life and its necessities. For Joe, however, life's possibilities were boundless. "Every day I go in the cab you never know what's going to
45 happen," he said, before adding: "I met you."

This doesn't seem such a big deal but I don't want to disappoint Joe so I take his number and promise to be in touch should anything arise. "It's about never giving up," he says as I fumble to find the fare. "You never give up. It's all about having dreams and dreams come true."

50 I don't believe Joe, and I don't believe Joe believes Joe, though I do believe in the power of dreams. It's fashionable to sneer at America's tenacious belief in the self-made man but I liked Joe's attitude. It was not the attitude of other cab drivers who seem to have resigned themselves to fate, such an un-American spirit. In that respect, Joe was the Last American Cab Driver after all.

55 Only when the taxi was out of sight did I realise that he hadn't given me my change.

Adapted from an article in *The Sunday Herald*

QUESTIONS

                                                                                                    Marks Code

1. According to the first paragraph (lines 1–6), visitors to New York and residents of New York have different attitudes towards travelling in taxi-cabs.

   In your own words, say what each attitude is and explain what has given rise to it.   **4 U**

2. "They are the kind of drivers that are imported for the purpose of scaring you witless. It works." (lines 5–6)

   What aspect of these sentences makes them effective?   **1 A**

3. *(a)* In paragraph 2 (lines 7–10), how does the writer emphasise the dangers of travelling by cab?   **2 U**

   (b) Why, then, did he choose to travel by cab on this occasion?   **2 U**

   (c) What **single word** used in paragraph 3 best suggests the pleasure the writer thought he would get from a taxi ride and how does it do so?   **2 A**

4. *(a)* How do New York cab drivers and their customers normally behave towards one another and how does the writer help you to work this out?   **2 A**

   (b) What suggested the writer's relationship with this driver would be different?   **1 U**

5. "At least, this was the alternative reality he had created for himself." (lines 22–23)

   (a) "Different life" means almost the same as "alternative reality".

   In what ways is "alternative reality" the more effective expression to use in this context?   **2 E**

   (b) What **facts** revealed in lines 24–39 suggest that the cab driver was deluding himself?   **2 U**

   (c) In lines 28–39, how does the writer make it seem as if we are listening to Joe telling his own story?   **1 A**

6. "For me, it seemed his story illuminated thwarted ambition and the inevitable compromise between the aims of life and its necessities." (lines 42–43)

   (a) In what way does the **register** used in this quotation contrast with that of most of the passage?   **1 A**

   (b) Explain with reference to the text how the cab driver's story "illuminated thwarted ambition and the inevitable compromise between the aims of life and its necessities".   **2 A**

7. *(a)* What do you think the writer means when he talks of "the power of dreams"? (lines 50–51)   **2 U**

   (b) In what way does the writer suggest the strength of the American belief in the self-made man in lines 51–54?   **1 A**

8. Why might the final paragraph (line 55) be considered an effective ending to the passage?   **1 E**

9. In this passage the writer is obviously trying to give a flavour of New York life in an entertaining way.

   By commenting on **at least two** techniques he uses, explain how well you think he has achieved his purpose.   **4 E**

[*END OF QUESTION PAPER*]   **Total (30)**

X039/202

NATIONAL
QUALIFICATIONS
2001

TUESDAY, 15 MAY
10.20 AM — 11.50 AM

ENGLISH AND
COMMUNICATION
INTERMEDIATE 2
Analysis and Appreciation

There are **two parts** to this paper and you should attempt both parts.

Part 1 (Textual Analysis) is worth 30 marks.

In Part 2 (Critical Essay), you should attempt **one** question only, taken from any of the Sections A–D.

Your answer to Part 2 should begin on a fresh page.

Each question in Part 2 is worth 30 marks.

NB You must not use, in Part 2 of this paper, the same text(s) as you have used in your Specialist Study.

PART 1—TEXTUAL ANALYSIS

Read the following short story and answer the questions which follow.

You are reminded that this part of the paper tests your ability to understand, analyse and evaluate the text.

The number of marks attached to each question will give some indication of the length of answer required.

You should spend about 45 minutes on this part of the paper.

THE VASE

The narrator of this short story is describing events on his last morning at home with his grandparents before going off to be a student at college for the first time.

I deliberately take a long time packing the rucksack. Had even taken out half of the clothes again so that my cassettes and tape recorder could lie amongst them to prevent damage. Toothbrush, paste and razor in the side pockets. Socks and pants. Asthma tablets, (it had recurred during a recent holiday in Scarborough) and hay fever tablets
5 (past the season but better to be safe). Thinking about the hair drier. No, I'll leave it for her though she'll probably never use it.

Derek should be arriving any moment in the Morris Traveller for a lift to the station, though he could be late. He usually is. The problem is whether to go through for a chat or just stay here. No point; just sit tight and wait for the horn.

10 My room was always dark, even on the brightest days, but today it seems dull beyond belief. The huge oak wardrobe sickens me utterly. I wanted rid of it for years and now it's rid of me. Funny. Wondering what the new room will be like. Probably very practical—yes, practical: chair, desk, bed, cupboard. That'll do fine.

Room C43, Tower block. Enough said.

15 I hear a noise outside and seconds later she calls from the other side of the door to tell me that Derek has arrived. I grab the rucksack and go quickly to the living room. Outside the window I can see the grass has been newly cut for the last time this year, the lawnmower still standing outside the hedge. Derek is sitting in the Morris on the other side of the road. The old man has just come in from the garden and he stands
20 next to my grandmother to say goodbye. I reach out my hand, which he takes firmly, when his face breaks from the strain of keeping something in, and after hurriedly stuffing a fiver into my pocket, he walks quickly into the kitchen and out into the garden.

We move out into the hall and she hasn't said anything yet but her cheeks are wet and
25 she seems somehow shrunken. I tower above her with one arm round her shoulder, the other dangling the rucksack inches off the floor. She tells me to take care son, and I tell her I will, I will, and I'll be back to see you once I've settled in and that but I can't cry. Not really. She is turning to open the front door when I hoist the rucksack clumsily onto my shoulder and it just catches the edge of the blue china vase which stands on top
30 of the display cabinet. Her wedding gift. We both turn to watch it falling slowly through space to smash on the hard linoleum of the hallway, and whilst she cries out it doesn't matter son, it doesn't matter, I am already out the door and running towards the car.

As we are pulling away, I look round for one last time and I see the old man struggling to put the lawnmower into the garden shed and her face is at the window, staring.

Jimmy Glen

QUESTIONS

Marks

1. Read lines 1–6.

   Select three items he packs, or considers packing, which tell us important things about his lifestyle or personality. State what each decision reveals about his lifestyle or personality. **3**

2. (a) What impression are you given of his bedroom (lines 10–12)? **1**

   (b) By commenting on **two** examples of word-choice in lines 10–12, show how this impression is created. **2**

3. How do the sentence structure **and** punctuation in lines 12–13 help you to follow his thinking? **4**

4. What impression do you get of his new room from its title "Room C43" (line 14)? **1**

5. Look at the actions of the narrator's grandfather in lines 19–23.

   Choose **one** expression which particularly helps you to understand what the old man was feeling and say why you have chosen it. **2**

6. Look at the conversation between the narrator and his grandmother (lines 26–27).

   How does the sentence structure give you the idea that this conversation takes place very quickly? **2**

7. Explain why the vase is described as "falling slowly through space" (lines 30–31). **1**

8. All through this story there are clues which show that this parting is going to be difficult.

   (a) Go back to the first sentence of the story.
   Why do you think that the narrator "deliberately" took a long time? **1**

   (b) There are other clues in the passage that the parting is going to be difficult.
   Choose **two** of these clues which have not been covered in other questions and show how they point to the parting being sad. **4**

9. In this short story there are three main characters.

   By selecting **one** significant detail for each character, explain **how successful** you think the writer has been in establishing their feelings.

   You may use material that has been used elsewhere in your answers. **6**

10. (a) The short story is called "The Vase".
    Explain the significance of the vase in the story. **2**

    (b) How does the writer highlight the importance of the vase? **1**

    Total (30)

[*Turn over for* PART 2—CRITICAL ESSAY

PART 2—CRITICAL ESSAY

Attempt ONE question only, taken from any of the Sections A to D. Write the number of the question you attempt in the margin of your answer book.

In all Sections you may use Scottish texts.

You must not use the extract from the Textual Analysis part of the paper as the subject of your Critical Essay.

You are reminded that the quality of your writing and its accuracy are important in this paper as is the relevance of your answer to the question you have attempted.

You should spend about 45 minutes on this part of the paper.

Begin your answer on a fresh page.

SECTION A—DRAMA

1. Choose a character from a play who has a human weakness such as jealousy, selfishness, pride, lack of self-knowledge, or any other human failing.

    How does the character's human failing affect the events of the play and one other character in the play?

    In your answer you must refer to the text and to at least **two** of: characterisation, plot, climax, theme or any other appropriate feature.

2. Choose a play in which at least one of the main characters is female.

    Show what important contribution the female character you have chosen makes to the action of the play.

    In your answer you must refer to the text and to at least **two** of: plot, key scenes, climax, structure or any other appropriate feature.

3. Choose a play which has a dramatic final scene.

    Show how successful you feel the ending of the play to be in tying up the plot and sorting out the characters' problems.

    In your answer you must refer to the text and to at least **two** of: climax, characterisation, dialogue, plot, structure or any other appropriate feature.

SECTION B—PROSE

4. Choose a character from a novel or short story who seems to you to be unfortunate in life, or for whom the ending is unhappy.

    Show how much of the character's misfortune you feel is caused by his or her own personality and how much by other circumstances in the short story or novel.

    In your answer you must refer to the text and to at least **two** of: characterisation, plot, structure, theme or any other appropriate feature.

5. Choose a short story in which suspense or tension is created.

    Show how this suspense or tension is built up and what effect it has on your appreciation of the short story.

    In your answer you must refer to the text and to at least **two** of: structure, language, plot, climax or any other appropriate feature.

6. Choose a prose work of fiction or non-fiction in which the setting is important.

    Show how the setting in time and/or place contributes to your enjoyment of the work.

    In your answer you must refer to the text, to the setting, and to at least **two** of: theme, ideas, the use of detail, imagery or any other appropriate feature.

SECTION C—POETRY

7. Choose a poem in which an incident or a character or an experience is vividly described.

   Briefly state what the poem is about, and go on to show how the techniques used make the description vivid.

   In your answer you must refer to the text and to at least **two** of: word-choice, imagery, mood, structure, characterisation or any other appropriate feature.

8. Choose a poem which makes you think more deeply about some aspect of life.

   State what aspect of life the poem deals with and show how the techniques used by the poet have deepened your understanding.

   In your answer you must refer to the text and to at least **two** of: theme, ideas, word-choice, imagery or any other appropriate feature.

9. Choose a poem which makes you feel pity or sympathy for a person or animal.

   Show how both the content and style of the poem create pity or sympathy.

   In your answer you must refer to the text and to at least **two** of: characterisation, word-choice, structure, tone or any other appropriate feature.

SECTION D—MASS MEDIA

10. Choose a film which you enjoyed for its story line but which depends a lot on special effects for its success.

    Show how the special effects were used to increase your enjoyment of the film.

    In your answer you must refer to the text and to at least **two** of: plot, editing, computer-generated images, animation, soundtrack or any other appropriate feature.

11. Choose a TV drama, series or serial which takes place in an everyday setting, such as a school, a hospital, a police station, or a neighbourhood.

    Show how media techniques are used to create a sense of drama or tension on screen.

    In your answer you must refer to the text and to at least **two** of: editing, use of camera, structure, lighting, action, soundtrack or any other appropriate feature.

12. Choose an opening sequence from a film which is immediately effective in holding your attention and establishing information vital to your understanding of the film.

    By analysing this sequence show how it is effective in establishing important elements of the film.

    In your answer you must refer to the text and to at least **two** of: editing, use of camera, opening graphics/titles, special effects, soundtrack or any other appropriate feature.

[END OF QUESTION PAPER]

[BLANK PAGE]

INTERMEDIATE 2 2002

X039/201

NATIONAL QUALIFICATIONS 2002

THURSDAY, 16 MAY 9.00 AM – 10.00 AM

ENGLISH AND COMMUNICATION
INTERMEDIATE 2
Close Reading

You should attempt all questions.

The total value of the Paper is 30 marks.

The passage which follows is adapted from "A Walk in the Woods" by Bill Bryson.

Read the passage carefully and then answer **all** the questions, **using your own words as far as possible**.

The questions will ask you to show that:

you understand the main ideas and important details in the passage—in other words, **what** the writer has said (**Understanding—U**);

you can identify, using appropriate terms, the techniques the writer has used to get across these ideas—in other words, **how** he has said it (**Analysis—A**);

you can, using appropriate evidence, comment on how effective the writer has been—in other words **how well** he has said it (**Evaluation—E**).

A code letter (U, A, E) is used alongside each question to identify its purpose for you. The number of marks attached to each question will give some indication of the length of answer required.

In this extract from his book "A Walk in the Woods", Bill Bryson tells of his reaction to some of the books he read before beginning his walk along the Appalachian Trail in North America.

Through long winter nights in New Hampshire, while snow piled up outdoors and my wife slumbered peacefully beside me, I lay saucer-eyed in bed reading clinically precise accounts of people gnawed pulpy in their sleeping bags, plucked whimpering from trees, even noiselessly stalked (I didn't know this happened!) as they sauntered unawares down
5 leafy paths or cooled their feet in mountain streams. People whose one fatal mistake was to smooth their hair with a dab of aromatic gel, or eat juicy meat, or tuck a chocolate bar in their shirt pocket for later, or in some small, inadvertent way irritate the olfactory properties of the hungry bear. Or, come to that, whose fatal failing was simply to be very, very unfortunate—to round a bend and find a moody male blocking the path, head
10 rocking appraisingly, or wander unwittingly into the territory of a bear too slowed by age or idleness to chase down fleeter prey.

Now it is important to establish right away that the possibility of a serious bear attack on the Appalachian Trail is remote. To begin with, the really terrifying American bear, the grizzly—*Ursus horribilis* as it is so vividly and correctly labelled—doesn't range east of
15 the Mississippi, which is good news because grizzlies are large, powerful and ferociously bad-tempered. Nothing unnerved the native Americans more than the grizzly, and not surprisingly since you could riddle a grizzly with arrows—positively porcupine it—and it would still keep coming. Even later hunters with big guns were astounded and unsettled by the ability of the grizzly to absorb volleys of lead with barely a wobble.

20 If I were to be pawed and chewed—and this seemed to me entirely possible, the more I read—it would be by a black bear, *Ursus americanus*. There are at least 500,000 black bears in North America, possibly as many as 700,000. They are notably common in the hills along the Appalachian Trail (indeed, they often *use* the trail, for convenience), and their numbers are growing. Grizzlies, by contrast, number no more than 35,000 in the
25 whole of North America, and just 1,000 in the mainland United States principally in and around Yellowstone National Park. Of the two species, black bears are generally smaller (although this is a decidedly relative condition: a male black bear can still weigh up to 650 pounds) and unquestionably more retiring.

Black bears rarely attack. But here's the thing. Sometimes they do. All bears are agile, cunning and immensely strong, and they are always hungry. If they want to kill you and eat you, they can, and pretty much whenever they want. That doesn't happen often, but—and here is the absolutely salient point—once would be enough.

So let us imagine that a bear does go for us out in the wilds. What are we to do? Interestingly, the advised tactics are exactly opposite for grizzly and black bear. With a grizzly, you should make for a tall tree, since grizzlies aren't much for climbing. If a tree is not available, then you should back off slowly, avoiding direct eye contact. All the books tell you that if the grizzly comes for you on no account should you run. This is the sort of advice you get from someone who is sitting at a keyboard when he gives it. Take it from me, if you are in an open space with no weapons and a grizzly comes for you, run. You may as well. If nothing else, it will give you something to do with the last seven seconds of your life. However, when the grizzly overtakes you, as it most assuredly will, you should fall to the ground and play dead. A grizzly may chew on a limp form for a minute or two, but generally will lose interest and shuffle off. With black bears, however, playing dead is futile since they will continue chewing on you until you are considerably past caring. It is also foolish to climb a tree because black bears are adroit climbers and you will simply end up fighting the bear in a tree.

To ward off an aggressive black bear, the books suggest making a lot of noise, banging pots and pans together, throwing sticks and rocks, and "running at the bear". (Yeah, right. You first, Professor.) On the other hand, they then add judiciously, these tactics could "merely provoke the bear". Well, thanks. Elsewhere they suggest that hikers should consider making noises from time to time—singing a song, say—to alert bears to their presence, since a startled bear is more likely to be an angry bear, but then a few pages later caution that "there may be danger in making noise", since that can attract a hungry bear that might otherwise overlook you.

The fact is, no one can tell you what to do. Bears are unpredictable, and what works in one circumstance may not work in another. In 1973, two teenagers, Mark Seeley and Michael Whitten, were out for a hike in Yellowstone when they inadvertently crossed between a mother and her cubs. Nothing worries and antagonises a female bear more than to have people between her and her brood. Furious, she turned and gave chase—despite the bear's lolloping gait it can move at up to 35 miles an hour—and the two boys scrambled up trees. The bear followed Whitten up his tree, clamped her mouth round his right foot, and slowly and patiently tugged him from his perch. (Is it me, or can you feel your fingernails scraping through the bark?) On the ground, she began mauling him extensively. In an attempt to distract the bear from his friend, Seeley shouted at it, whereupon the bear came and pulled him out of his tree, too. Both young men played dead—precisely the wrong thing to do, according to all the instruction manuals—and the bear left.

I won't say I became obsessed by all this, but it did occupy my thoughts a great deal in the months while I waited for spring to come. My particular dread—the vivid possibility that left me staring at tree shadows on the bedroom ceiling night after night—was having to lie in a small tent, alone in an inky wilderness, listening to a foraging bear outside, and wondering what its intentions were.

Adapted from *A Walk in the Woods* by Bill Bryson

QUESTIONS

Marks Code

1. What might have caused the writer to be "saucer-eyed" (line 2)?   1 U

2. "reading clinically precise accounts of people gnawed pulpy" (lines 2–3)

    Considering this expression **as a whole**, explain fully how the language used makes it humorous.   2 A

3. "(I didn't know this happened!)" (line 4)

    (a) Explain the use of the brackets round this expression.   1 A

    (b) Explain the use of the exclamation mark.   1 A

4. (a) What do "aromatic gel", "juicy meat" and "a chocolate bar" (line 6) have in common that attracts bears?   1 U

    (b) Which single word used later in the same paragraph **makes this clear**?   1 U

5. **In your own words**, explain the ways in which human beings might have **accidental** confrontations with bears.   2 U

6. Read lines 12–32 again.

    (a) **In your own words**, outline the points the writer makes to support his contention that, if he were attacked by a bear, it is more probable "it would be by a black bear".   3 U

    (b) **In your own words**, what characteristic of black bears makes even an attack by them unlikely?   1 U

7. "*Ursus horribilis* as it is so vividly and correctly labelled" (line 14)

    Why has Bryson used the word "labelled" in this expression instead of a word like "called"?   2 A

8. Why might "positively porcupine it" (line 17) be considered an effective expression here?   2 E

9. Read paragraph 4 (lines 29–32) again.

    Identify any **one** technique used by the writer in this paragraph and explain how this technique helps him to create an appropriate tone.   2 A

10. Give the meaning of the word "adroit" and explain how lines 45 and 46 help you to work it out.   2 A

11. (a) What "tactics" are you advised to adopt if you are attacked by a black bear?   2 U

    (b) Quote an expression which suggests that Bryson is not convinced of the wisdom of this advice.   1 U

12. Explain clearly Bryson's main purpose for including the story of the two teenagers, Mark Seeley and Michael Whitten.   2 A

Think about the passage as a whole.

13. Bill Bryson is a very popular writer of travel books.

    Referring in detail to at least two techniques he uses in this passage, explain why people might find his writing enjoyable.   4 E

Total (30)

[*END OF QUESTION PAPER*]

X039/202

NATIONAL
QUALIFICATIONS
2002

THURSDAY, 16 MAY
10.20 AM – 11.50 AM

ENGLISH AND
COMMUNICATION
INTERMEDIATE 2
Analysis and Appreciation

There are **two parts** to this Paper and you should attempt both parts.

Part 1 (Textual Analysis) is worth 30 marks.

In Part 2 (Critical Essay), you should attempt **one** question only, taken from any of the Sections A–D.

Your answer to Part 2 should begin on a fresh page.

Each question in Part 2 is worth 30 marks.

NB You must not use, in Part 2 of this Paper, the same text(s) as you have used in your Specialist Study.

PART 1—TEXTUAL ANALYSIS

Read the following poem and answer the questions which follow.

You are reminded that this part of the Paper tests your ability to understand, analyse and evaluate the text.

The number of marks attached to each question will give some indication of the length of answer required.

You should spend about 45 minutes on this part of the Paper.

In this poem, the poet finds a dead rat which, among other things, makes him think of the possibility of his own death.

RAT

My hand discovers you—a scrap
of doormat with claws, scrubbingbrush
with teeth, among leaves, old sacks
in the world's most unlit outhouse.
5 I am a bellows that sucks the air,
as the breath rushes into me
like a hunted thing, scared
of you, and of what you are not.
Hardened to the brittle, the literal
10 emblem of yourself. That pebble
embedded in your side is more
alive in its cool, smooth silence.
With a stick, I pick you up
by a tail as still as a coathook.
15 Did death catch you on the hop
old enemy—as it catches those
who make a habit of survival?
I won't pick up that, I think.
Then your eyeless eye's fullstop
20 stops me—mid-life, mid-thought—
with the riddle of your dry reminder.
I shut my eyes as I throw you
as far as I can throw your image
out of my mind's out-of-sight.
25 One morning, I'll find you there
grinning at me, like to like,
from your delicate skeleton.

Brian McCabe

QUESTIONS

Marks

1. In the opening lines (1–4) the poet describes his discovery of the rat.

    (a) Which of his senses is most clearly involved at the moment of discovery? **1**

    (b) Choose one of the metaphors in these lines which deals with this sense and say how effective the metaphor is in highlighting the sense of horror. **3**

    (c) What does the description of the place where he found it add to your feelings about the experience? How does it do so? **3**

2. Read lines 5–8.

    (a) What is his physical reaction to the rat? **1**

    (b) Choose **two** examples of word-choice **or** imagery and explain how the poet makes this reaction clear to you. **4**

3. The appearance of the dead rat has not changed much—it still looks outwardly like a rat. What, however, has changed? (lines 9–10) **1**

4. What is unusual about the use of the word "alive" in line 12? **2**

5. Read lines 15–17.

    (a) What is the question which the poet imagines asking the rat? Answer in your own words. **1**

    (b) Why do you think the poet describes the rat as "old enemy"? **1**

6. How does the poet's use of the phrase "pick . . . up" in line 13 differ from his use of it in line 18? **3**

7. Read lines 19–21.

    (a) What causes the poet to stop? **1**

    (b) Explain how one of the techniques the poet uses in these lines helps to make the moment dramatic. **3**

8. How does line 24 reinforce the poet's depth of feeling as he throws the rat away? **2**

9. By referring to ideas **and** word-choice, explain fully what the poet conveys to you in the final three lines. **4**

Total (30)

[Turn over for PART 2—CRITICAL ESSAY

Official SQA Past Papers: Intermediate 2 English 2002

PART 2—CRITICAL ESSAY

Attempt ONE question only, taken from any of the Sections A to D. Write the number of the question you attempt in the margin of your answer book.

In all Sections you may use Scottish texts.

You must not use the poem from the Textual Analysis part of the Paper as the subject of your Critical Essay.

You are reminded that the quality of your writing and its accuracy are important in this Paper, as is the relevance of your answer to the question you have attempted.

You should spend about 45 minutes on this part of the Paper.

Begin your answer on a fresh page.

SECTION A—DRAMA

1. Choose a play which deals with an important human issue: for example war, crime, teenage rebellion, family conflict, or any other issue which you regard as important.

   Say what the issue is and go on to show how two or more of the characters in the play deal with the issue.

   In your answer you must refer to the text and to at least **two** of: theme, characterisation, plot, key scene(s), or any other appropriate feature.

2. Choose a play in which one of the characters achieves his or her aim or ambition.

   State what the character's aim or ambition is and go on to identify what aspects of his or her personality help him or her to overcome the obstacles in the way of success.

   In your answer you must refer to the text and to at least **two** of: characterisation, key scene(s), climax, plot, or any other appropriate feature.

3. Choose a play in which a conflict between two characters, or between two sets of opinions, is an important element in the play.

   Show what this conflict is, why it is important, and how it is resolved, or not, at the end of the play.

   In your answer you must refer to the text and to at least **two** of: characterisation, theme(s), key scene(s), climax, or any other appropriate feature.

SECTION B—PROSE

4. Choose a novel or short story which deals with a powerful human emotion: for example love, shame, hatred, fear, embarrassment, despair, joy, or any other strong emotion.

   Show how the emotion you have chosen affects one, or more than one, of the characters, and go on to show how it affects the course of the story.

   In your answer you must refer to the text and to at least **two** of: characterisation, structure, tone, language, or any other appropriate feature.

5. Choose a novel or a short story in which one of the characters has to struggle with difficulties in order to reach a satisfactory outcome.

   Outline the difficulties which face the character you have chosen and show how her or his strengths or weaknesses affect the course of the story and how a satisfactory ending is finally reached.

   In your answer you must refer to the text and to at least **two** of: characterisation, climax, dialogue, plot, or any other appropriate feature.

SECTION B (continued)

6. Choose a prose non-fiction work which by its use of detailed and vivid description of scenes and events increases your understanding and appreciation of what is going on.

   You should outline the scenes and events and go on to show how the detailed description makes it vivid for you and increases your understanding and appreciation of what is happening.

   In your answer you must refer to the text and to at least **two** of: setting, key scene(s), characters, language, or any other appropriate feature.

SECTION C—POETRY

7. Choose a poem where the poet starts off by describing an everyday happening or incident and then goes on to make a deeper or more serious point about human nature by the end of the poem.

   Briefly describe the starting point of the poem and state what you think is the serious point made by the end. Now go on to show how the poet's use of poetic techniques deepens your understanding of the poem.

   In your answer you must refer to the text and to at least **two** of: theme, structure, word-choice, tone, or any other appropriate feature.

8. Choose a poem about childhood, or teenage years, or motherhood, or families, or the world of work, or old age.

   Show how the poet, by choice of content and skilful use of techniques, helps you to imagine what it is like to be at any one of these stages in life.

   In your answer you must refer to the text and to at least **two** of: word-choice, imagery, ideas, characterisation, or any other appropriate feature.

9. Choose a poem which creates an atmosphere of fear, or mystery, or celebration, or sadness.

   Show how the poet builds up this atmosphere and show how it heightens your appreciation of the poem.

   In your answer you must refer to the text and to at least **two** of: imagery, sound effects, word-choice, tone, or any other appropriate feature.

SECTION D—MASS MEDIA

10. Choose a film which has a powerful scene in which a strong human emotion such as love or hate or terror is portrayed.

    Show how the emotion of the scene is important to the theme of the film, and how the emotion is emphasised for you by the filmic techniques used.

    In your answer you must refer to the text and to at least **two** of: use of camera, sound effects, editing, music, or any other appropriate feature.

11. Choose a TV drama, series or serial which seems to deal mainly with themes reflecting the less pleasant aspects of life.

    Show how a theme of this kind is dealt with in such a way as to help your understanding of the aspect of life shown.

    In your answer you must refer to the text and to at least **two** of: content, characterisation, editing, setting, or any other appropriate feature.

[*Turn over for Question 12 on Page six*]

SECTION D (continued)

12. Choose a film or TV series which has some elements of fantasy or of the supernatural, or of science fiction.

Show how the director manages to use one of these elements to make the film or series enjoyable for you.

In your answer you must refer to the text and to at least **two** of: use of camera, special effects, editing, animation, or any other appropriate feature.

[END OF QUESTION PAPER]

INTERMEDIATE 2 2003 SQP

[C115/SQP208]

NATIONAL
QUALIFICATIONS

Time: 1 hour

ENGLISH
INTERMEDIATE 2
Close Reading
Specimen Question Paper
(for examinations in and after 2003)

Answer all questions.

30 marks are allocated to this paper.

Read the passage carefully and then answer **all** the questions, **using your own words as far as possible**.

The questions will ask you to show that:

you understand the main ideas and important details in the passage—in other words, **what** the writer has said (**Understanding—U**);

you can identify, using appropriate terms, the techniques the writer has used to get across these ideas—in other words, **how** he has said it (**Analysis—A**);

you can, using appropriate evidence, comment on how effective the writer has been—in other words, **how well** he has said it (**Evaluation—E**).

A code letter (U, A, E) is used alongside each question to identify its purpose for you. The number of marks attached to each question will give some indication of the length of answer required.

The passage that follows is adapted from a newspaper article advising scientists how to improve their image.

How to make science loveable

Scientists have been attacked for being too remote. Brian Millar explains how they can win back public support.

"Pay attention," winks Jennifer Aniston in the shampoo ads. "Here comes the science bit." Of course we don't pay attention during the science bit, and Jennifer doesn't expect us to. Few of us paid attention in school during the science bits and fewer still pay attention as adults.

5 Small wonder then that scientists are trusted less than ever before, and are perceived as failing to provide straightforward answers to pressing questions over issues such as BSE and GM foods.

If it's any consolation to scientists, they're not alone. Almost every institution in the UK has seen a significant drop in public confidence over the last decade. The police, the 10 church and the legal system have all taken serious knocks. Confidence in the press has also managed to decline steeply.

Some years ago it was big corporations who had to acknowledge the power that individual consumers had over them. Now it's scientists' turn to feel that the public are turning on them. But they should beware of talking to slick admen about glossy 15 campaigns, and here I speak as a slick adman. Scientists aren't a brand to be packaged and given a superficial makeover. Because of modern politics, we all have highly developed spin detectors. We might tolerate a bit of hype from a shampoo. We won't in a politician or public figure.

It will take more than a new logo on a letterhead and some nice TV spots to change the 20 public's perception of scientists. And the change has to come from scientists themselves.

Luckily, scientists are naturally great communicators—with each other. The sharing of information is culturally ingrained into scientists as with no other community.

They just don't get out enough or rather, they're not allowed out. Science is hierarchical in a way that few other organisations are anymore. The voices that we hear 25 tend to be either senior academics or PR hacks from large corporations.

There's little or no opportunity for the public to come into contact with the workers at the coal face, the people who might give us the answers we're looking for and not toe the party line. Where do you think you'd get a more satisfactory picture of the safety of Sellafield? The visitor's centre? Or the pub down the road where the boffins knock off 30 for a swifty after work? Exactly.

Now pay attention: here comes the marketing bit. Today, markets are conversations. A revolution is happening in the communications industry: ad copywriters like me are standing back and watching as real people talk to real people. The scandal! Check out any website on books. Most of the reviews there are written by the readers. Last time I 35 looked, one of the Harry Potter novels had more than 2,000 reader comments, and comments on the comments. Every one of them was more honest and informative than the blurb on the back cover.

In my experience, conversations with scientists are always interesting, especially after a few beers. They have the same concerns as the rest of us: they worry about the food 40 their kids eat or whether mobile phones are toasting their brains.

But because they paid attention during the science bit, they are better equipped to answer those questions than the rest of us who chose the gentler path of humanities subjects, with their clean classrooms and chairs with proper lumbar support (what is it with scientists and lab stools?).

45 And when they're tackling those questions in a pub, boffins leave the science bit alone because otherwise they see our eyes glaze over. They speak to our concerns as individuals. They generalise. They speculate. They are not rigorous in their explanations. They become unscientific—like the rest of us.

It's that insight that we need when we are wondering what's lurking in a pack of frozen
50 burgers. That's when we need the voice of somebody who's like us, but who can pronounce "spongiform encephalopathy".

So where should this great conversation between science and the rest of us take place? The internet. It is a perfect medium for public conversation. Ironically it was invented by scientists, to help them spread ideas more efficiently. Now the rest of us have caught
55 up and filled their lovely web full of pop group tribute sites.

The internet is no respecter of hierarchy: news postings by a junior scientist or a 10-year-old kid can sit alongside those of a Nobel Prize winner. The pecking order is different: if you make valid points, if you're entertaining or funny, you get attention. Word spreads: she's interesting; this stuff is unbelievably tedious; this site tells you how
60 Jennifer gets her hair like that.

Of course thousands of conversations with scientists will offer up a much more complex range of views for us to digest, from the rational to the downright eccentric. But we make daily judgements about who we trust and who we don't as part of everyday life. We can take one more in our stride.

65 Do Nobel Prize winners and busy post-doctorate researchers really have the time to hang out on web discussion pages, answering questions from teenagers and loony conspiracy theorists? Bill Gates does. How does this start? Not with formal bodies. The last thing we need is a lovely pristine chat room at the Royal Institution. It needs to come from the 25-year-old who sets him/herself up as thenakedchemist.com (still
70 available), and hundreds and thousands of others. Starting conversations online is easy. Asking and answering questions is easy. If you were bright enough to get a chemistry degree, you can build yourself a website right now and start changing the world. It's not rocket science.

Adapted from an article in *The Telegraph*

QUESTIONS

Marks Code

1. Read the first paragraph (lines 1–4).

   Having considered what the rest of the paragraph says, why do you think Jennifer Aniston winks as she tells us to "pay attention"?   1 U

2. How does the inclusion of the expression "perceived as" (line 5) change the meaning of the sentence in which it appears?   2 A

3. What does the writer mean by an "institution" (line 8), and how does the rest of the paragraph (lines 8–11) help you to understand what he means?   2 A

4. Read lines 12–18.

   (a) Giving examples which support your answer, explain how the writer's choice of words underlines his distrust of what he calls "admen".   2 A

   (b) **In your own words**, explain what "modern politics" has helped us to develop.   2 U

5. **In your own words**, according to lines 19–25,

   (a) what fact about scientists should help them to improve their image?   2 U

   (b) what fact about scientists might make it difficult for them to improve their image?   2 U

6. Read lines 31–37.

   (a) In the first sentence of this paragraph, the writer echoes the opening of the passage. Why do you think he does this?   1 A

   (b) "The scandal!" (line 33)

   What effect does the writer seem to be aiming for in this sentence? What techniques does he use to try to achieve it?   3 A

   (c) **In your own words**, what exactly does the writer describe as a "scandal"?   2 U

7. (a) Which of the following possibilities is true according to lines 41–44?

   The writer believes that studying science is

   A   more important
   B   more dangerous
   C   more difficult
   D   more profitable

   than studying the humanities subjects.   1 U

   (b) How does the writer make this clear?   2 A

8. How does **the structure** of the paragraph in lines 45–48 add to its impact?   2 A

9. (a) What is ironic about suggesting the internet as a means for scientists to communicate with ordinary people?   2 U

   (b) The writer argues that the internet is the best means for scientists to communicate with ordinary people.

   Referring closely to what he says in the final three paragraphs, clearly explain the arguments that you find most convincing.   4 E

[END OF SPECIMEN QUESTION PAPER]   Total (30)

[C115/SQP208]

NATIONAL QUALIFICATIONS

Time: 1 hour 30 minutes

ENGLISH
INTERMEDIATE 2
Critical Essay
Specimen Question Paper
(for examinations in and after 2003)

Answer **two** questions.

Each question must be taken from a different section.

Each question is worth 25 marks.

Answer TWO questions from this paper.

Each question must be chosen from a different Section (A–E). You are not allowed to choose two questions from the same Section.

In all Sections you may use Scottish texts.

Write the number of each question in the margin of your answer booklet and begin each essay on a fresh page. You should spend about 45 minutes on each essay.

The following will be assessed:

- **the relevance of your essays to the questions you have chosen**
- **the quality of your writing**
- **the technical accuracy of your writing.**

Each answer is worth up to 25 marks. The total for this paper is 50 marks.

SECTION A—DRAMA

1. Choose a scene from a play in which a character makes an important decision.

   Say what causes him or her to make the decision and go on to show how the decision affects his or her actions in the rest of the play.

   In your answer you must refer to the text and to at least **two** of: key scene, characterisation, structure, or any other appropriate feature.

2. Choose a play in which one of the characters suffers a breakdown in a relationship with another character.

   Show what the relationship was and go on to explain what makes it break down.

   In your answer you must refer to the text and to at least **two** of: characterisation, key scene(s), climax, or any other appropriate feature.

3. Choose a play in which one of the main concerns is injustice or cruelty or exploitation or betrayal.

   State the main concern and go on to show how the playwright deals with this concern in such a way as to involve your sympathies.

   In your answer you must refer to the text and to at least **two** of: theme, characterisation, key scene(s), or any other appropriate feature.

SECTION B—PROSE

4. Choose one or more prose works (novel, short story(ies), essay(s), journalism) which deal(s) with family or community life.

   Show how differing points of view in the family or community are developed in the work(s) you have chosen, and how they have influenced your thinking.

   In your answer you must refer to the text and to at least **two** of: theme, structure, conflict, or any other appropriate feature.

5. Choose a novel or a short story in which there is an obvious climax or turning point.

   Show how the writer leads up to this turning point or climax, and say what its significance is for the rest of the story.

   In your answer you must refer to the text and to at least **two** of: structure, plot, key incident(s), or any other appropriate feature.

6. Choose a prose work of fiction or non-fiction which creates a sense of time and place.

   Show how the sense of time and place is created and evaluate its importance in your appreciation of the main concerns of the prose work.

   In your answer you must refer to the text, and to at least **two** of: setting, language, theme, or any other appropriate feature.

SECTION C—POETRY

7. Choose a poem which deals with a happy experience.

   Briefly describe the experience and show how the poet has communicated the feelings of happiness by the use of various poetic techniques.

   In your answer you must refer to the text and to at least **two** of: word choice, tone, imagery, structure, or any other appropriate feature.

8. Choose a poem which increased your understanding of any aspect of life in the modern world.

   State what aspect of life in the modern world the poem illustrates and go on to show how the poem, both by its content and by its style, increased your understanding.

   In your answer you must refer to the text and to at least **two** of: ideas, theme, imagery, word choice, or any other appropriate feature.

9. Choose a poem which deals with a particular time of year.

   Show how the poet, by her or his choice of content and skilful use of techniques, helps you to appreciate the positive or negative aspects of the time of year described.

   In your answer you must refer to the text and to at least **two** of: word choice, imagery, tone, ideas, or any other appropriate feature.

SECTION D—MASS MEDIA

10. Choose a film which has an important sequence involving thrilling action such as a chase, a fight, an ambush, or a supernatural event.

    Briefly say why the sequence is important, and show how the sequence is made exciting for the audience.

    In your answer you must refer to the text and to at least **two** of: use of camera, mise-en-scène, editing, music, or any other appropriate feature.

11. Choose a TV drama, series or serial which has a political, social, or religious theme.

    Show how the portrayal of this theme is enhanced by the characters and setting of the drama, series or serial.

    In your answer you must refer to the text and to at least **two** of: content, characterisation, mise-en-scène, or any other appropriate feature.

12. Choose a TV series or serial which depends to some extent for its success on humour.

    To what extent do you feel the series or serial to be successful because of its humour of situation, or character(s), or both?

    In your answer you must refer to the text and to at least **two** of: setting, characterisation, editing, plotting, or any other appropriate feature.

SECTION E—LANGUAGE

13. Choose an aspect of spoken language which you have identified in one age group or locality.

    Outline how you gathered your evidence and which aspects of spoken language you focused on. Go on to show the main characteristics of the language you identified, and assess the advantages and disadvantages of these characteristics for communication.

    You must refer to specific examples of speech, and to at least **two** features such as: register, accent, dialect, vocabulary, or any other appropriate feature.

14. Choose aspects of language which are commonly used to persuade the reader to think or act favourably towards a particular organisation or group of people.

    Show how in the course of your investigation you gained an awareness of the effectiveness of the techniques used to influence you.

    You must refer to specific examples and to at least **two** features such as: register, tone, or any other appropriate feature.

15. Choose an aspect of communication (TV, radio, internet, etc) which has made an impact on language within the last twenty years. Explain, with reference to examples you have studied, how you think language has changed and whether you think it has affected the accuracy of communication.

    You must refer to specific examples and to at least **two** features such as: register, vocabulary, codes, abbreviation, or any other appropriate feature.

[*END OF SPECIMEN QUESTION PAPER*]

But it is the wind—the endless shifting gradients of atmospheric pressure—that makes travelling in a small boat into an *adventure*, in the sense defined by the dictionary ("That which happens without design; chance, hap, luck"). The wind blows you into places that you'd never meant to visit, and keeps you pinioned there. The wind is a mad travel agent, with a malicious and surrealist turn of wit. You want to go to France—the wind will maroon you for ten days in Dover. You want to go to the Shetland Islands, and the wind will make you spend a week in Bridlington as penance for your vanity. You can't move without the wind's consent, and when you do move, you find yourself suddenly rescheduled, headed for a destination that you hadn't heard of ten minutes ago. Every day the chart and the pilot book produce surprises; and if you have any sense, you always take the wind's advice and go where it listeth, to the obscure village or small town that offers shelter. Sometimes you have to stay out at sea, missing your original destination altogether. More often, you're driven in haste into harbours you'd overlooked, far short of where you'd planned to be that night.

Going by sea is a reliably constant adventure. It's a slow and unpredictable business. It requires patience and a curiosity about those unregarded places in the world where you're forever finding yourself stranded. Since its original circuit of the British Isles, *Gosfield Maiden* has taken me to Ireland, France, Belgium, the Netherlands, West Germany, Denmark and Sweden. In every country, the wind has taken control of the itinerary, landing the boat up, for days on end, in ports that I had no idea I was destined to visit.

From Girvan in Scotland to Hogänas in Sweden, they were chosen by the weather, these windfall-landfalls. It is true about any port in a storm: as you round the inner breakwater after a few hours out in a rough sea, the dingiest town seems a wonderful place to be. I've come humiliatingly close to kissing the stones of Grimsby fish dock, I was so glad to be there. The worse the weather, the more you love the town—which is useful, since you'll probably have time to learn the name of every single street before the wind will allow you to leave it.

Adapted from *For Love and Money* by Jonathan Raban

QUESTIONS

Marks Code

1. (a) Explain clearly why the writer "wandered down the Mississippi" in his boat. **2 U**

   (b) Explain fully how the evidence the writer provides shows that there was "no element of stunt" in the trip. **2 U**

2. (a) What **two** reasons does the writer give for feeling that he had become "an accredited river man" (line 11)? **2 U**

   (b) What word in the second paragraph (lines 6–13) suggests that the "society of the river" (line 6) has its own history and tradition? **1 A**

3. Quote **two** expressions from the first two paragraphs (lines 1–13) which convey the notion of a leisurely journey and experience. **2 A**

4. (a) In your own words, describe the writer's reasons for thinking he was "through with boats" (line 15). **2 U**

   (b) Quote **two** expressions from lines 20–25 which suggest that the writer nevertheless missed both the boat and the river. **2 A**

5. What is the effect of the writer's use of **alliteration** in ". . . a succession of soft, suburban outings." (line 25)? **1 A**

6. "I've found a way of keeping on the move that works . . ." (line 31)

   (a) Explain in some detail any **two** of the writer's reasons for believing this. **4 U**

   (b) Comment on the sentence structure used in presenting these reasons. **2 A**

7. The purpose of lines 41–54 is to illustrate how **the wind** makes travelling in a small boat an adventure.

   Giving an example to support your answer, explain how the writer has used either sentence structure **or** imagery to do this. **2 A**

8. ". . . the wind has taken control of the itinerary . . ." (lines 59–60)

   Quote **two** other expressions the writer uses in lines 55–61 to convey this idea. **2 A**

9. "It is true about any port in a storm:" (line 63)

   How effective do you find the final paragraph in elaborating on this idea?

   You may wish to consider any **one** feature such as structure, word choice or illustration. **2 E**

10. The writer's main purpose in this extract is to convey his fascination with travelling by boat.

    Identify **two** features of style the writer uses and comment on how well you believe he has achieved his purpose. **4 E**

Total (30)

[END OF QUESTION PAPER]

X115/202

NATIONAL
QUALIFICATIONS
2003

FRIDAY, 16 MAY
2.20 PM – 3.50 PM

**ENGLISH
INTERMEDIATE 2**
Critical Essay

Answer **two** questions.

Each question must be taken from a different section.

Each question is worth 25 marks.

Answer TWO questions from this paper.

Each question must be chosen from a different Section (A–E). You are not allowed to choose two questions from the same Section.

In all Sections you may use Scottish texts.

Write the number of each question in the margin of your answer booklet and begin each essay on a fresh page. You should spend about 45 minutes on each essay.

The following will be assessed:

- **the relevance of your essays to the questions you have chosen**
- **the quality of your writing**
- **the technical accuracy of your writing.**

Each answer is worth up to 25 marks. The total for this paper is 50 marks.

SECTION A—DRAMA

1. Choose a play which has an important scene at a turning point in the play.

    Give a brief account of the scene and go on to show why it is important in the play as a whole.

    In your answer you must refer to the text and to at least **two** of: key scene, structure, characterisation, conflict, or any other appropriate feature.

2. Choose a play which explores relationships within a family, or between two members of a family.

    Describe any such relationship(s) and go on to show how they affect the events of the play.

    In your answer you must refer to the text and to at least **two** of: characterisation, plot, theme, conflict, or any other appropriate feature.

3. Choose a play which deals with an issue of importance to society today.

    State what the issue is and go on to show how, through the plot and characters, the play increased your understanding of this issue.

    In your answer you must refer to the text and to at least **two** of: theme, plot, characterisation, dialogue, or any other appropriate feature.

SECTION B—PROSE

4. Choose a novel or short story where one of the main characters is female.

   Show how the character's contribution to the content and outcome is important in the story as a whole.

   In your answer you must refer to the text and to at least **two** of: characterisation, theme, structure, plot, or any other appropriate feature.

5. Choose **one** or **more than one** work of fiction **or** non-fiction which deals with a serious aspect of life.

   State what this serious aspect is and go on to show how your understanding of it was deepened by your reading of the work(s).

   In your answer you must refer to the text and to at least **two** of: theme, conflict, characterisation, setting, or any other appropriate feature.

6. Choose a novel or short story which has an incident or moment of great tension.

   Describe briefly what happens at this point in the story and go on to show how it is important for the outcome of the story as a whole.

   In your answer you must refer to the text and to at least **two** of: structure, key scene, characterisation, climax, or any other appropriate feature.

SECTION C—POETRY

7. Choose a poem in which a particular place is described, either in the town or in the country.

   Briefly state what the poem is about and then go on to show how the techniques highlight particular aspects of the place, making it seem real to you.

   In your answer you must refer to the text and to at least **two** of: imagery, word choice, structure, tone, or any other appropriate feature.

8. Choose a poem which creates an atmosphere of despair about human existence.

   Show how the poet, by his use of ideas and techniques, leaves you with a pessimistic feeling about life.

   In your answer you must refer to the text and to at least **two** of: mood, word choice, tone, imagery, or any other appropriate feature.

9. Choose a poem in which you find the ending particularly interesting or surprising or satisfying.

   By considering the whole poem say why you think the ending is effective.

   In your answer you must refer to the text and to at least **two** of: structure, ideas, imagery, word choice, or any other appropriate feature.

[Turn over

SECTION D—MASS MEDIA

10. Choose an important scene from a film in which an atmosphere of mystery, or horror, or suspense is created.

    Briefly state what happens in the scene and why it is important to the film as a whole. Go on to show what techniques are used to create the atmosphere of mystery or horror or suspense.

    In your answer you must refer to the text and to at least **two** of: editing, use of camera, characterisation, soundtrack, or any other appropriate feature.

11. Choose a TV drama, series or serial which creates a picture of a community.

    Show how this picture is created and is made realistic for you.

    In your answer you must refer to the text and at least **two** of: sets, characterisation, theme, editing, or any other appropriate feature.

12. Choose a film in which the closing sequence makes use of a variety of film techniques to make its dramatic impact.

    Briefly state what happens in the closing sequence and show how the techniques used make the ending dramatic.

    In your answer you must refer to the text and to at least **two** of: editing, music, use of camera, soundtrack, or any other appropriate feature.

SECTION E—LANGUAGE

13. Consider language which is designed to persuade the reader of the benefits of a product or the rights of a cause.

    Show how in the course of your investigation you gained an awareness of the emotive nature of the language you were dealing with and evaluated its effectiveness.

    You must refer to specific examples, and to concepts such as register, tone, intonation or any other appropriate feature.

14. Consider aspects of spoken language which you have identified in **one** or **more than one** group of people.

    Outline how you gathered your evidence. Go on to show the main similarities and/or differences you identified within the group or between groups, and what conclusions you drew from your findings.

    You must refer to specific examples of speech, and to language concepts such as register, accent, dialect, vocabulary or any other appropriate feature.

15. Consider the language specific to a group which has a common leisure or vocational interest.

    Show to what extent technical terminology used by the group is useful in describing concepts accurately.

    You must refer to specific examples, and to concepts such as technical terminology, jargon, abbreviation or any other appropriate feature.

[*END OF QUESTION PAPER*]